Lends a Hand

by Daphne Greaves

SCHOOL PUBLISHERS

Cover, ©Mary Steinbacher/PhotoEdit; p.3, ©Envision/Corbis; p.4, ©Alamy; p.6, ©Chev Willkinson/ Getty Images; p.10, ©Jack Hollingsworth/Getty Images; p.11, ©Robert Holmes/Corbis; p.12, ©Patrick Ward/Corbis; p.13, ©Getty Images.

Printed in China

ISBN 10: 0-15-350532-X
ISBN 13: 978-0-15-350532-4

Ordering Options
ISBN 10: 0-15-350334-3 (Grade 4 Below-Level Collection)
ISBN 13: 978-0-15-350334-4 (Grade 4 Below-Level Collection)
ISBN 10: 0-15-357526-3 (package of 5)
ISBN 13: 978-0-15-357526-6 (package of 5)

2 3 4 5 6 7 8 9 10   985   12 11 10 09 08 07

Characters

Ramon	Alicia
Mama	Lucia
Mrs. Garcia	Abuelo
Papa	Mr. Johnson
Mr. Montez	Jack

Setting: The courtyard of the Hibiscus Arms, a garden apartment building, where people are preparing for a party

Ramon: Corn fritters, my favorite!

Mama: Are your hands clean?

Ramon: Yes, Mama.

Mrs. Garcia: Let's see. Oh, yes, these hands are gorgeous. Here's your reward.

Ramon: Thank you, Mrs. Garcia. Mama, I came over to help with the cooking for the party.

Mrs. Garcia: What do you do to help?

Ramon: My chores consist of peeling vegetables and cleaning shrimp. I grate cheese and coconut. I do anything Mama wants.

Mrs. Garcia: Your mother is very lucky to have a helper like you.

Mama: Yes, I am. Many aspects of Ramon's personality are just like his father's. Thank you for offering to help, Ramon, but the cooking is done.

Mrs. Garcia: That's true. Mrs. Lopez has made chicken and rice. Mr. Alfonso has taken care of the beans. Your mother has made the salads and her delicious desserts.

Mama: Mrs. Hernandez has made her remarkable shredded beef.

Ramon: I guess I missed my opportunity to help.

Mama: Why don't you see if your father needs a hand setting up the music?

Ramon: Thanks, Mama. That's a great idea.

Ramon: *Hola*, Papa!

Papa: Hello, son.

Mr. Montez: Hello, Ramon. I almost did not recognize you!

Ramon: Hi, Mr. Montez.

Mr. Montez: Are you ready to dance salsa today? As I recall, you're an excellent dancer.

Ramon: Thank you.

Papa: Be sure to ask your sister to dance today.

Ramon: Oh, Papa, do I have to?

Papa: Yes, you have to.

Mr. Montez: What's the matter? Does she have two left feet? Afraid she'll step on your toes?

Ramon: Alicia is a good dancer. She just doesn't like dancing with me.

Papa: That's not true.

Ramon: Papa, Alicia doesn't want anything to do with me these days.

Papa: She's just going through a big sister thing. Still, you be a good brother and ask her to dance.

Ramon: Yes, Papa.

Mr. Montez: Before anyone dances, we have to move these speakers.

Ramon: Let me help you.

Papa: No, these speakers are too heavy for you.

Ramon: I want to help, too. What can I do?

Mr. Montez: Please be careful, son. We don't want the misfortune of an accident.

Papa: It would be suitable to go help your sister with the decorations.

Ramon: But Papa—

Papa: Go on, she won't bite.

Ramon: Yes, Papa.

Alicia: I chose all the decorations for a reason, Lucia. The fruits symbolize the sweetness of life.

Lucia: What do the flowers symbolize?

Alicia: Beauty. Lucia, just hang up the flowers, not the hearts. Remember, we're going for an effect that's festive and not too ornate.

Lucia: I remember.

Alicia: Ramon, you're going to tear that pineapple!

Ramon: I am not!

Alicia: What are you doing here anyway?

Ramon: Dad told me to come over here to join your little decorating huddle. What do you intend to use this flower for?

Alicia: Ramon! Leave that flower alone! Just don't touch anything.

Ramon: But I want to help.

Alicia: We don't need your help. Right, Lucia?

Lucia: Thanks, Ramon, but we've got it covered.

Ramon: Papa said I should help you with the decorations.

Alicia: That's not fair! The Tenants Group selected me to be in charge of decorations.

Ramon: Well, Lucia's helping you.

Alicia: That's because Lucia understands what I want. Right, Lucia?

Lucia: Right. The paper fruit goes in the middle of the tables. The plastic flowers get hung from the trees.

Ramon: I can do that.

Alicia: You know very well you never do anything I say.

Abuelo: Ramon!

Ramon: Maybe if you weren't so bossy all the time—

Lucia: Ramon, your grandfather is calling you.

Abuelo: Ramon! Come here, please.

Ramon: Coming, Abuelo!

Ramon: Yes, Abuelo?

Abuelo: You remember my friend, Mr. Johnson.

Ramon: Hello, Mr. Johnson. How are you?

Mr. Johnson: I'm fine, Ramon. Your grandfather is teaching me to play dominoes. He's a great teacher. He plays vigorously, which means I'd better play my last domino quickly. I win!

Abuelo: Maybe I'm too good of a teacher. Ramon, this is Mr. Johnson's grandson, Jack.

Ramon: Hi, nice to meet you, Jack.

Jack: Hello, Ramon.

Abuelo: Mr. Johnson and I are going to play another game.

Mr. Johnson: I'm ready!

Abuelo: I wouldn't grin so expectantly if I were you. You still have a lot to learn about dominoes.

Mr. Johnson: We'll see about that.

Abuelo: Why don't you take Jack and give him some *guarapo*?

Ramon: Sure, Abuelo. Come on, Jack.

Jack: What's *guarapo*?

Ramon: It's a drink made from fresh squeezed sugarcane juice.

Jack: Mmm . . . this is good. How come you call your grandfather *Abuelo*?

Ramon: It's the Spanish word for "grandfather."

Jack: Oh, I see. Your abuelo said there's going to be a big party here today.

Ramon: Every year, the people have a party in the courtyard. We eat great Cuban food, listen to Cuban music, dance, and play games.

Jack: Why is everything Cuban?

Ramon: Most of the people here made the journey from Cuba. My dad says it's a way to reconstruct the life they had in Cuba. It's also a lot of fun.

Jack: Sounds like it. Sounds like a lot of work, too.

Sugarcane

Ramon: Yes, but everyone pitches in. My mom made a lot of the food. My dad is setting up the music. My sister is putting up the decorations. You see, everyone helps.

Jack: What did you do?

Ramon: Me? Well . . . I uh—

Mama: Ramon! There's my right-hand helper! I've been looking all over for you. I need you to borrow some folding chairs.

Ramon: Where should I get them?

Mama: I suggest you make your destination the Community Center next door.

Ramon: Right away, Mama!

Jack: Hey, Ramon! May I help, too?

Ramon: Sure, Jack. Like I said, everyone helps at our parties.

Think Critically

1. What details does the author give about Cuban food?

2. What is the meaning of the word *vigorously* on page 11?

3. What did Ramon do after his father said he couldn't help set up the speakers?

4. How does Ramon feel about asking his sister to dance?

5. Do you think Ramon will be a good worker when he grows up? Explain your answer.

 **Social Studies**

Learn More Use a world atlas to find out more about the country of Cuba. Locate Cuba on a map. What state is it closest to? What body of water surrounds it? Make a list of facts you find about Cuba in the atlas.

School-Home Connection Plan a family party. What kind of food, music, and decorations would you choose?

Word Count: 1,004